Catalina Magdalena Hoopensteiner Wallendiner Hogan Logan Bogan Was Her Name

Catalina Magdalena Hoopensteiner Wallendiner Hogan Logan Bogan Was Her Name

by
TEDD ARNOLD

SCHOLASTIC INC. Cartwheel BOOKS®

New York Toronto London Auckland Sydney
Mexico City New Delhi Hong Kong Buenos Aires

To Imogene, Charlie, Carol, Cathy, John, and Judy—
I've learned so much from all of you, this song included.
—T.A.

ISBN 0-439-67849-8

12 11 10   8 9 10/0

Printed in the U.S.A.   40

First Scholastic paperback printing, October 2004

She had a funny name, but she wasn't much to blame;
Her mother gave it to her just the same, same, same.

Catalina Magdalena Hoopensteiner Wallendiner
Hogan Logan Bogan was her name.

Well, she had two peculiar hairs on her head;
One was black and one was red.

Catalina Magdalena Hoopensteiner Wallendiner
Hogan Logan Bogan was her name.

She had two eyes that were quite a sight;
One looked left and the other looked right.

Catalina Magdalena Hoopensteiner Wallendiner
Hogan Logan Bogan was her name.

She had two holes in the bottom of her nose—
One for her fingers…

...and one for her toes.

Catalina Magdalena Hoopensteiner Wallendiner
Hogan Logan Bogan was her name.

She had two teeth inside of her mouth;
One went north and the other went south.

Catalina Magdalena Hoopensteiner Wallendiner
Hogan Logan Bogan was her name.

She had two arms that flopped all around;
When she walked, they would drag on the ground.

Catalina Magdalena Hoopensteiner Wallendiner
Hogan Logan Bogan was her name.

She had two feet that were wide and flat—
Each one bigger than a bathroom mat.

Catalina Magdalena Hoopensteiner Wallendiner
Hogan Logan Bogan was her name.

She had one brain inside of her head;
What it thought is what she said.

Catalina Magdalena Hoopensteiner Wallendiner
Hogan Logan Bogan was her name.

We love you, sweetie.

Some folks say her breath smells sweet;
But me, I'd rather smell her feet.

Catalina Magdalena Hoopensteiner Wallendiner
Hogan Logan Bogan was her name.

If rain makes flowers sweet and clean,
There oughta be a downpour on Magdale-e-e-n!
O-o-o-o-o-o-o-h—

Catalina Magdalena Hoopensteiner Wallendiner
Hogan Logan Bogan SMITH was her name.

What was her name again? Almost everyone who sings this old camp song has his own set of verses and a slightly different name for Catalina. I *know* that my version of her name is the correct one because that's how I first heard it—from a sweet young girl, Carol, who became my wife. It was before we were married and it was dinnertime at her family's house. When they asked what kind of salad dressing I wanted, innocently I answered, "Catalina." Everyone at the table looked at each other, smiled, and burst into song: "Oh-h-h, Catalina Magdalena Hoopensteiner Wallendiner Hogan Logan Bogan was her name!" I thought they were insane! Then just a few years ago when Carol and I were in California, we gazed out over the Pacific Ocean and asked our host the name of the island that was visible on the horizon. We were told, "Catalina." Carol and I looked at each other, smiled, and burst into song. That's when I decided that I *had* to make this book. My very informal research has led me to believe that the song enjoyed popularity in the 1940s and later, particularly at church youth camps, but I can't say how old it actually is. Many improvisational verses have likely never been written down. And the vagaries of the meter are as you might expect from around the campfire. Here are just a few other versions of Catalina's name that I've heard. I'm sure you've heard others. Enjoy!

She had two eyes that were quite a sight.

One looked left and the oth-er looked right.

Chorus

Cat-a-li-na Mag-da-le-na Hoop-en-stein-er Wall-en-di-ner

Ho-gan Lo-gan Bo-gan was her name.

Madalina Catalina Rupesteena Wanna Donna Hoko Poko Poko was her name.

Agdalina Magdalina Hopataka Wakataka Hoka Moka Poka was her name.

Madalina Catalina Whoopastina Wilamina Oopsy Doopsy Woopsy was her name.

Aggalina Maggalina Whoops Now Whoops Now Ooga Booga Booga was her name.

Mac-a-lena Mac-a-lena Rubenstine Walk-a-dime Hokey Pokey Loca was her name.

Catalina Magdalena Hoopensheimer Wobbleheimer Hogan Bogan Logan was her name.

Matalina Catalina Hoopsa-scotta Walka-dotta Hoka Loka Poka was her name.

Magalena Hagalena Oooka Wakka Takka Wakka Oka Moka Poka was her name.